POLITICS OF PLACE

SURFSIDE CONDO TRAGEDY

A PROVOCATIVE NEW SERIES

ENLARGED PRINT EDITION

By Activist Author Diane Freaney

Politics of Place: Surfside Condo Tragedy, First Edition

Published by Emerson House Press

Author Photo by Carson's Tavern

ISBN: 978-1-957365-13-8 (e-book)

ISBN: 978-1-957365-14-5 (paperback)

US Copyright Registration No.: TX 9-322-146

www.dianefreaney.com

POLITICS OF PLACE

SURFSIDE CONDO TRAGEDY

A PROVOCATIVE NEW SERIES

Foreword by Commissioner Eula Clarke, City of Stuart

[Introduction Commissioner Clark arrived on the Treasure Coast in 1987 and knows more history than anyone regarding the City of Stuart and Martin County, except Alice L. Luckhardt, City of Stuart historian.

Commissioner Clarke is very thorough, often interrupted by difficult legal cases. I am confident her forward will be worth waiting for, in the event it doesn't make this First Edition.

—Diane Freaney]

Preface

The Florida Legislature stole my thunder and passed _**Senate Bill 4D –**_
**Building Safety Act for Condominium and Cooperative Associations,** in
special session May 23-25, 2022. _SB 4D_ is 88 pages long and written in
legalese so most folks will never read it. However, buyers are demanding
information—not just financial which they are already entitled to under
the law—but information on inspections, insurance, loans, mortgages and
liens on the property, and answers to virtually any questions they want to
ask. Good realtors and good lawyers are making sure buyers get
everything they ask for - or risk their licenses.

My purpose in writing this book is to put forth workable solutions to
problems that make most folks roll their eyes and say "good luck with
that."

The Florida Legislature enacted laws to solve my "good luck with that"
problems and went further than I dreamed possible when I began writing
this book.

I move on to the work of Dr. Martin Luther King Jr., a brilliant strategist
who was responsible for the framework of some of the most profound
legislation in the United States since the Constitution. Dr. King was a
master collaborator, and always knew the right time to seek common
ground, embrace new relationships and speak out on a subject he once
avoided.

Dr. King passed in 1968, just five years after condominiums became a thing
in Florida. Perhaps outcomes would have been different in community
housing if Dr. King had lived to a natural old age.

I want to acknowledge Miami-Dade Circuit Judge Michael Hanzman for his wisdom and caring in crafting a fair settlement. For his ability to get lawyers to work together to get the largest settlement for the 98 people who perished, while assuring that no one at Champlain Towers South was left wanting. For his ability to understand and explain the financial aspects of the law, a unique ability for lawyers in my experience.

1 The Hon. Michael Hanzman, judge for the Eleventh Judicial Circuit Court, Civil Division, in Miami-Dade County, Florida

There were a cadre of superheroes at Champlain Towers South that fateful morning June 24, 2021 and for several months afterward. It would be impossible to name them all here. Miami-Dade Circuit Judge Michael Hanzman is the Superhero Extraordinaire. In my opinion, his work on the Champlain Towers South Tragedy will change the work of lawyers, accountants, insurance and mortgage companies, and other construction and building professionals for the future and will keep ordinary citizens safe in their homes.

Table of Contents

Senate Bill 4D – Building Safety Act for Condominium and Cooperative Associations

Proceed with Caution

The average condo dweller/buyer is on high alert and will be demanding much more from their condo board, realtors, accountants, lawyers and other professionals associated with community associations. At the same time, reputable community association professionals have their dance cards full, often with long waiting lists to take on new clients. And no reputable professional will cut corners these days, after seeing the long list of professionals associated with Champlain Towers South that each contributed millions of dollars to the billion-dollar-plus settlement.

SB 4D only applies to condominiums over three stories, excluding thousands of two story condos, most of those in the affordable housing category. Folks who live or want to live in the two story category want the same assurances that are available to folks in high-rises.

I have already seen change happen in my Martin County Over 55 Condo. The condo board has taken steps that only three months ago they said they would never take.

Building Inspections

- Inspections of condominiums three stories in height and above will be required when the buildings reach 30 years of age (as determined by occupancy certificate) and then every 10 years thereafter.

- For condominiums within three miles of the coast, the first required inspections will be when the buildings reach 25 years of age and then every 10 years afterward.

- For buildings occupied before July 1, 1992, the first inspections must be completed by Dec. 31, 2024.

- There will be two phases to inspections. If a visual inspection by a licensed architect or engineer authorized to practice in Florida reveals no signs of substantial structural deterioration, no further action is necessary until the next required inspection. If structural deterioration is detected, a second phase of testing is required to determine whether the building is structurally sound.

Reserve Studies and Funding for Structural Reserves

- Mandatory reserve study and funding for structural integrity components (building, floors, windows, plumbing, electrical, etc.).

- Condo associations will no longer be able to waive cash-reserve requirements for structural work.

Mandatory Transparency

- Provide all owners and residents access to building safety information.

Condo Board Members

- Condo board members who neglect to raise needed money and undertake repairs can henceforth be sued by condo owners for dereliction of duty.

Developer Requirements

- Clear developer requirements for building inspections, structural integrity reserve study, and funding requirements prior to transition to the residents.

- Required reserve study will cover load-bearing walls, primary structural elements, roofs and foundations, among other things, and could reduce the chances that construction or design defects are passed on to owners.

Florida DBPR and Local Municipalities

- Engagement of the Florida Department of Business and Professional Regulation (DBPR) and local municipalities to track condominium buildings and the inspection reporting.

Florida Building Commission

The Florida Building Commission, a department of the Florida DBPR, oversees Florida Building Codes, which are widely recognized as the best in the United States. According to an March 18, 2018 article by Gloria Gonzalez in Business Insurance, "**Florida's building codes deemed strongest, Delaware weakest,**" Florida had the highest score for its building codes at 95 – compared to its 2015 score of 94 – and rose to the top of the list."

The article goes on to say, "States with strong, updated codes saw stunning proof this year in Florida that updated, well-enforced building codes have led to the construction of homes and buildings that can stand up to fierce hurricane winds," Julie Rochman, CEO and president of Insurance Institute for Business & Home Safety, said in a statement. "It can't be any clearer: these codes work. Unfortunately, many states took no action to improve their code systems and a few have weaker systems in place now than they had in 2015."

First Non-Profit Housing Cooperative
in the United States

Finnish Home Building Association

In 1916, Finntown became the site of the first non-profit housing cooperative in the United States when the Finnish Home Building Association built two cooperative houses, named Alku and Alku Toinen (translated respectively to "Beginning" and "Beginning Second" at 816 and 826 43rd Street, in Brooklyn.

2 Alku Toinenin Sunset Park, Brooklyn

By 1922, the Finns had constructed twenty co-ops in Sunset Park. These initially catered primarily to the area's Finnish population, but others of

European descent also lived in these co-ops. In honor of the Finnish community that inhabited Sunset Park, a block of 40th Street, in front of the Imatra Society building at 740 40th Street, was co-named "Finlandia Street" in 1991.

Immigrant Tribes

Immigrants tended to cluster together in tribes, bringing cultural values from "the old country," while seeking freedom and a different lifestyle in the new country. Sunset Park was a middle, residential neighborhood, settled by the Irish (1840), followed by Polish and Nordic Americans in the 19th century, and the Italians in the 20th century. The first Norwegians, Swedes, and Danes were maritime workers who settled near the waterfront, while Finns were mostly tenant farmers or non-landowning laborers. (Source: Wikipedia)

Non-Profit Housing Cooperatives

The Finnish Home Building Association non-profit housing cooperatives looked more like Dr. Martin Luther King Jr.'s cooperative business model than the 501(c) non-profits of today. Middle class families got together, designed and built homes in the same neighborhood. Dr. King advocated for the civil rights of his tribe, black Americans. The Finns were white as were all the Nordic tribes. White folks were just not on Dr. King's radar, although, I believe he loved all people.

Dr. Martin Luther King, Jr.

Dr. Martin Luther King Jr. was a smart businessman, in addition to being a brilliant strategist and a pastor, a servant of God. One of the strategies that Dr. King and the Civil Rights Movement used—and that those who advocate for racial and economic justice still favor—is the cooperative business model.

The Cooperative Business Model

Dr. King believed in folks coming together to own and control their own businesses, people can create stable jobs, build community wealth and inspire democratic participation.

Alberta Coop in Portland, Oregon

I discovered the Alberta Coop when I lived in Portland Oregon. I encourage you to check out the Alberta Coop website if you want to learn more about the coop business model.

As a CPA, I was most impressed with the clear and concise explanation of how the coop accounting model and how I, as a coop member owner, fit into that picture.

The Alberta Coop uses a QuickBooks accounting system. I am not a fan of Quickbooks but this system works well for the Alberta Coop. I think I recall that the system was developed internally by a worker owner.

I considered running for the Board and attended an in-person meeting. The meeting dragged on for hours and I knew it was not for me. Now all meetings are on Zoom and the agenda and minutes are posted online.

Connect Credit Union

I needed a bank where I could cash checks when I moved to Stuart, Florida. Connect Credit Union 1993 S. Kanner Highway was on my route so one day I stopped in and opened an account. The staff is competent and helpful and I always get to speak with a person, either on the phone or in person when I stop at the bank.

Connect Credit Union is for personal banking only, something I discovered the hard way. My first royalty payment for the Emerson House Press came into my CCU account and was immediately sent back. I needed to have a business checking account for royalty payments.

In my business career, I had worked for Citibank, and, as Treasurer of a publicly traded company, was the primary contact for the BIG BANKS my company used.

I am confident Dr. King would have been an advocate of credit unions.

International Minds in Finland (IMIF)

In December 2016, a Finnish academic group, International Minds in Finland (IMIF), asked me to make a presentation. I asked the IMIF host, "Why me?" He told me they liked my ideas for building strong communities. I told him many of my ideas came from studying Finland. A copy of this presentation can be found in the Appendix.

What is a 501(c)(4)?

In my opinion, 501(c)(4) is where the dark money hides. In a 2013 *Washington Post* article, Sean Sullivan gives two noteworthy examples:

> "Crossroads GPS, the conservative group co-founded by Karl Rove is one well-known example. On the other end of the political spectrum is Organizing for Action, which is what President Obama's campaign operation turned into after the 2012 election. Often, organizations will have multiple arms, including a nonprofit and a super PAC. American Crossroads, for example, is a super PAC affiliated with Crossroads GPS."

The US Tax Code, which was built by lobbyists, has become increasing complex, prompting Fareed Zakaria's comment that the US Tax Code is threatening our democracy.

"The U.S. tax system is not simply corrupt; it is corrupt in a deceptive manner that has degraded the entire system of American government." (Complexity Equals Corruption, Fareed Zakaria, *Time Magazine*, Oct. 31, 2011)

Condominium Associations

Dr. King's cooperative model makes membership meaningful by making members owners of a business. Condominium associations are businesses that need to generate revenue so they have adequate funds to maintain the property, including the common elements, for the benefit of the members and their guests.

Dr. King's model is a partnership model, not a non-profit model, with revenues and expenses accruing to each member based on percentage ownership in their unit and the common elements. Each member gets one vote, and the members elect a Board of Directors to serve them all.

Florida Condominium Act (1963)

As I began my research for this book, I decided to become a Licensed Community Association Manager (LCAM). The 16-hour Prelicensure class taught by <u>Fred Gray of Gray Systems Inc</u>. was an eye-opener for me. I thought I knew-it-all and, boy, did I learn a lot!

My family has owned Florida beach front properties since 1981 when my father purchased their first Over 55 Condo at Lake Harbour Towers East 801 Lake Shore Drive (Unit 118) in Lake Park, Florida.

Unit 118 came with a tenant on a long-term lease, which was just fine with my father. My parents were living in a one story single-family house with pool and walking distance to the beach on Singer Island, just over the bridge from Lake Park.

My father was a general contractor before he retired so he did his research before he purchased. As I recall, the developer had an excellent reputation building good concrete structures with good rebar, pilons driven deep, able to withstand the hundred year flood zone.

My father quickly got involved, first serving on the maintenance committee, then getting elected to the Board. In this days, engineers retired early with good pensions from General Motors and Ford and moved to Florida to escape the harsh winters in Detroit. These men (and they were all men in those days) volunteered their skills and their time to help with maintenance on the condominium property.

Bobby, the maintenance guy, would post days and times that volunteers were needed and the schedule would quickly fill up. The volunteer maintenance crew kept maintenance fees down and the property in tip top condition.

Unit 418 became available in 1986. My father snapped it up because he knew it was a good value, having served on the maintenance committee and the Board of Directors. In those days, the Board self-managed and did exactly what Chapter 718 Condominium Florida Statutes expected the Board to do.

My parents decided that the first floor was not ideal because of the prospect of climate change. Richard Allen and his sister Elizabeth, the long-term tenants were interested in purchasing the unit so my father sold it to them for $90,000, a gain of $9,000 in 1987. No bad, you say, but the Condo Board had been doing exactly what they were charged with doing: maintaining the property value by keeping current with the annual and deferred maintenance of the property.

My father gutted and renovated Unit 418 in 1987 before they moved in. The renovation mostly worked except both my parents smoked in the apartment. It may even have been legal then.

I purchased Unit 418 in 1997 from my mother after my father passed and my mother went to live in a nursing home. I do not smoke and was obliged to totally renovate and disinfect to make the condo unit fit for me to inhabit. My parents paid $95,000 for Unit 418 but it only appraised at $70,000 when I bought it, a victim of a slump in the real estate market and a smoke infested environment.

Times change and 801 Lake Harbour Towers East became embroiled in dodgy administrative management and elder abuse. I remember condo members organizing to get things back on track. The process felt like such an uphill battle.

Change did happen although not as the Condo members expected. A story for another day...

My Connection to Florida Seaside Properties

This book is like no other I have written. I spent many years flying in and out of Miami, visiting friends on Fisher Island, one of the wealthiest addresses in the United States. My friends were shopaholics and were always looking for new places to spend money.

We often stopped at one of the shiny new residential towers that were rapidly changing the skyline of Miami. Interior decorators relished the opportunity to furnish and adorn the sample apartments, creating next season's household decor. We may even have stopped in at Champlain Towers South on our way to Bal Harbour Shops, one of the highest grossing shopping malls in the world.

I could have visited Surfside when I visited family. My parents spent a month each year at the Sea View Hotel, 1.3 miles north of Surfside in Bal Harbour. The Sea View was "old Florida" which suited my parents just fine. My father's best story is that another guest mistook him for the pool boy and gave him a two dollar tip.

My family has been connected to Florida beach front properties since before I was born. My parent's met on St. Petersburg Beach, sneaking in some beach time between their busy seasonal jobs. My father was a bell hop at the Vinoy Park Hotel; my mother and my grandmother were soda jerks at a Woolworth's lunch counter.

3 Historic Vinoy Park Hotel, St. Petersburgh, FL

After "the season" ended, my mother and my grandmother went back home to Toronto and resumed their resort work at the Lake Country north of Toronto. My father went back to Boston, beginning his career selling fur coats.

My parents got married in Canada, and my mother emigrated to the United States to join my father. Money was tight and for a while, and beach vacations in Florida were on hold.

When I was about ten years old, my mother packed up us three kids and we visited my grandmother who now lived permanently in St. Petersburg, Florida. Granny lived in a small trailer parked in her landlord's driveway, with barely room for herself. We stayed in a rooming house, walking distance to St. Petersburg Beach.

Finally, my mother convinced my father to take a two-week vacation and come with us. From the beginning it was clear that my parents were looking for a place to vacation during "the season" and ultimately retire. We tried several beach front properties on the barrier island west of St Petersburg Beach. My sisters and I loved the white sand beaches with calm waters, great for kids to build sand castles.

Our parents were dreaming of a retirement without children. One year we drove to Fort Lauderdale to try out the East Coast beaches. My parents found the Sea View Hotel, a quiet oasis on the beach in an area known for its night life. My parents started vacationing at the Sea View Hotel for a month each year during "the season."

My father started watching the real estate ads for single family homes in Palm Beach County. He focused on Riviera Beach's Singer Island, a sleepy beach community nestled between the ocean and the intercostal waterway. He drove north for some open house viewings and settled on a one story three-bedroom, two-car garage house with a pool and citrus trees at 1151 Emerald Drive, on Singer Island.

My parents planned to retire the following year, so he purchased the house at 1151 Emerald Drive on April 1977 just before returning to Massachusetts at the end of "the season".

My father built our family home at 29 Sargent Road in South Weymouth, Massachusetts in 1950. It was his dream home, including an amazing basement party room and wonderful landscaping. They were sad to leave but the time had come to leave the ice and snow behind and move to sunny South Florida.

The house on Singer Island was perfect but also a lot of work. My father started looking immediately for a condominium in the area as the next step in their retirement plans.

Campbell Property Management

As often happens, an organization or an individual simplifies my research process as I start writing a new book. Campbell Property Management is that organization, the cream that rises to the top, for the Surfside Condo Tragedy.

From the Campbell Property Management website:

> "Company History: In 1953 **William B. Campbell Sr**. established **Campbell Property Management** after retiring from the New York Police Department and relocating to South Florida. Not one to sit idly on the beach, Bill began a small maintenance business serving vacation and rental properties and ultimately moved to buying, selling and managing rental apartments. In the 1970's, the conversion and development of condominiums began to take off and Campbell recognized the importance of professional management for the property and facilities. Thus an industry was born."

I found a **Request for Proposal** on the Campbell website and filled it in using Lakeside Pointe Apartment No. 5 Association, Inc. Click on Request for Proposal and up comes **Request Your Complimentary Consultation.**

> "We would look forward to the opportunity to discuss how we can save your association money and provide you better service. To request a free consultation, please fill out the form below."

I diligently filled in the form and, as promised, had a response in less than 48 hours from Ashley Dietz-Gray, Campbell's Marketing Director & Customer Relations Specialist.

To be accepted as a Campbell client, the Community (COA, HOA or Co-operative) has to have a minimum of 150 Units, Ashley told me. However, I was welcome to participate in Campbell's extensive education program.

WOW! I am not used to companies turning down business so this was an eye opener for me.

"Turning down business" seems to be the "new norm" post-Surfside for professionals working in the community association space. The "new norm" means higher membership costs— operating and reserves, and strict adherence to rules. Florida's building codes are among the best in the world, yet until *SB 4D*, signed into law on May 26, 2022 by Governor Ron DeSantis, Florida allowed too much "wiggle room" to thwart the rules.

> **DISCLAMER**: I do not now and have never worked for Campbell. I have availed myself of Campbell's free educational services, including free CEUs for my CAM Business and my personal LCAM. I have met other professionals that serve the community association field.

The United States of Florida

The matriarch of a fourth generation family sprinkler, wells and water pump business in Florida believes we need to start thinking of ourselves as the United States of Florida; i.e. Florida terrain and weather are different and require different construction processes than places "up north" or "out west" or "in the mountains" or "on the plains" or "in the dessert." Interestingly, Florida is almost there.

Florida Community Associations

In 2017, Florida had the highest number of community associations (48,000), inhabited by the highest number of residents (9,753,000) in the United States, according to the Community Association Institute. I am guessing that number is even higher now, five years later.

Community associations are the most basic level of government, required to follow federal, state, county, and municipal laws, the declaration, articles of incorporation and by-laws created by the developer and the rules and regulations created by the community association board. All this while dealing with a diverse group of full-time and seasonal residents, with different economic, family and lifestyle circumstances.

So much to consider. Where to start?

SIMPLIFY!

Who Pays the Billion Dollar Plus Settlement?

Securitas Security Services USA pays $517.50 Million

The company paying the biggest portion of the settlement -- $517.5 million -- is Securitas Security Services USA.

The firm's employees were contracted to provide guard services, monitor visitors in the lobby and operate the building's security system on an emergency basis, including the all-call alarm panel at the front desk to alert residents.

- Jay Weaver, Miami Herald

Shamoka Furman, the security guard on duty, called 911 twice and was credited with calling her residents on their phones.

The building security system, which should have announced loudly **"Leave The Building! Leave the Building!"** did not sound. Was it because Shamoka did know about the security system or because it was somehow disabled? Seven minutes is a long time, many folks believe there would have been fewer deaths if the alarm had sounded.

Eighty Seven Park Pays $400 Million

Eighty Seven Park, the building next door to Champlain Towers South in Miami Beach, pays $400 million into the settlement fund, with 40% coming from John Moriarty and Associates of Florida, the general contractor.

Building Restoration Professionals

The building construction, restoration and service professionals got hosed in the Champlain Towers South settlement, providing millions of dollars, mostly paid by their insurance.

Structural Engineering

The structural engineer for a condominium association has risen to the top as the most important professional. I watched *Painting Projects Planning Process CEU Webinar* (see resources: websites for link) and was surprised to hear that the paint committee must get a sign off from the condo's structural engineer before beginning to paint. The reason - the structural engineer must inspect for rust stains, mildew and other problems, and sign off before the paint job begins and covers up structural problems at least temporarily.

Wikipedia tells us that structural engineering dates back to 2700 BC and the building of the pyramids. Structural engineers are "trained to design the 'bones and muscles' that create the form and shape of man-made structures."

Morabito Consultants, the structural engineering firm for Champlain Towers South, was fined $16 million because a junior engineer was sent when the building manager (LCAM) requested an inspection of the crack in the planter on the pool deck. The junior engineer did not have adequate training and supervision to recognize the severity of the problem. The general feeling is that corrective action taken at that time may have prevented the collapse. I bet Morabito won't make that mistake again.

Building Code Administrators and Inspectors

Building inspectors generally work for local municipalities and are responsible for issuing certificates of occupancy (CO) when a project is complete and assuring that construction documents are available for future reference. The Surfside building inspectors were corrupt, issuing a CO to Champlain Towers South without adequate inspection or archiving construction records as legally required. In those days, municipal employees were often underpaid and made themselves a living wage through kickbacks from developers.

Today's building inspectors are well-qualified and expect to earn salaries commensurate with their experience. Professional building inspectors are in demand and can easily change jobs if they do not get the respect and renumeration they deserve.

Today the tools for comprehensive building inspections are well in reach of most municipalities and available for rent for smaller municipalities.

Post-Surfside, corruption and graft is not really an option.

Exterior Building Restoration

Western Waterproofing Company of America promotes its services on its website as "South Florida's Master Craftsmen in Building Envelope Restoration."

Western agreed to pay $25 million to the Champlain Towers South settlement. I am guessing because they did not sound the alarm and insist that work begin sooner and, in the meantime, provide support to the buckling pool deck from below.

Senate Bill 4D will keep Western fully employed for many years to come. I am betting their work from this point forward will be exactly what the owners and residents of Champlain Towers South deserved.

Concrete Restoration

Concrete Protection & Restoration, Inc. paid $11 million into the settlement. I am guessing because they did not sound the alarm and insist that the parking garage, the pool, the gym and the valet parking area be closed immediately and temporary supports be put in place.

Becker & Poliakoff Pays $31 Million

The *Sun Sentinel* article *Becker & Poliakoff law firm the 'nemesis' of condo safety reformers* by Brittany Wallman et al tells it all. I encourage you to read this article before you select a Board Certified Condominium and Planned Development Lawyer for your condominium association.

Alan Becker and Gary Poliakoff created and wrote the rules. Becker died in 2020 and Poliakoff died in 2014. In my opinion, it is time for Becker & Poliakoff (B&P) to cease to exist. I am sure B&P currently has some some good condominium attorneys. Other Florida attorneys will know who the good B&P attorneys are and snap them up. The remaining B&P attorneys should announce their retirement and surrender their bar membership.

Before Surfside, the only law firm I was aware of was Becker & Poliakoff and my experience with B&P was always negative. I will recount my negative experience with B&P attorneys in other books on the *Politics of Place* series. I keep excellent records and will provide documentation.

I am grateful to Judge Hanzman and the team of attorneys he assembled to orchestrate the over $1 billion settlement. I am confident that this settlement signals a new era for the Florida legal profession.

Florida Institute of CPAs

The Champlain Towers South settlement list has no Certified Public Accounting firm listed. CPA firms are usually the "fall guys," so many firms have ceased to exist after a major scandal.

This fact positions small local State of Florida CPA firms to take a leadership position in designing and implementing systems post-Surfside.

Florida Statutes 2022

SB 4D 2022

Senate Bill 4D - Building Safety Act for Condominium and Cooperative Associations contains some profound changes. The Florida legislature promises to continue working to include more changes as constituents find what works and what needs further clarification.

Right now Florida Statues have five separate categories for planned communities:

- 718 Condominiums

- 719 Cooperatives

- 720 Homeowners Associations

- 721 Vacation and Time Share Plans

- 723 Mobile Home Park Lot Tenancies

My Recommendation

Combine the five categories into one category. I favor condominium since it seems to be the most common name for planned communities in the United States.

The differences between the planned communities can be addressed in the documents, initially prepared by the developer and transitioned to the planned community from the developer during turnover.

Why change?

Simple!

Make it easy for planned community members, board members, community association managers, accountants and lawyers to understand.

SB 2D 2022

Senate Bill 2D - signed into law by Florida Governor Ron DeSantis on May 26, 2022. The summary description:

> "Property Insurance; Creating the Reinsurance to Assist Policyholders program to be administered by the State Board of Administration; requiring certain property insurers to obtain coverage under the program; revising homeowner eligibility criteria for mitigation grants; requiring claimants to establish that property insurers have breached the insurance contract to prevail in certain claims for damages; requiring the Office of Insurance Regulation to aggregate on a statewide basis and make publicly available certain data submitted by insurers and insurer groups, etc. APPROPRIATION: $150,000,000"

Most folks feel *SB 2D* may cause property insurance cost increases to level off and perhaps decrease a little but not for at least 12 to 18 months.

In the meantime, we all need to pray for fewer major weather events.

Florida Association Documents

Essentially the residential association developer is the founding father (or mother) of a new government unit. Association members become citizens of this new governmental unit, in addition to being citizens of the United States, the State of Florida, the county and the city, town or unincorporated area where the association is located.

The developer prepares the initial association documents and records the documents with the county clerk in the public records where the residential association is located.

Recently the legal profession has been encouraging older community associations (thirty to fifty year old) to redo their community association documents. The quoted cost, usually $7,500 to $10,000, is staggering for most community associations, particularly in light of the *SB 4D* requirement to beef up reserves and the recent increases in the cost of property & casualty insurance.

My Recommendation

Start Fresh

Eliminate the old declaration, articles of incorporation and by-laws created by the developer, with periodic update by the community association. Simply archive the old docs and move on.

Create a new standard declaration, standard articles of incorporation and standard by-laws, based on the best thinking of Florida condominium professionals today and blessed by Florida Bar Condominium and Planned Development Law group of the Real Estate, Probate & Trust Section.

Standard Docs Available for Condos of 150 Units or More

Condominiums of one hundred and forty-nine (149) and less need not apply.

However, smaller condominiums may choose to give up their individual ownership and become part of a larger condominium group in their neighborhood.

For example, my Palm Beach County condo of twenty units is part of a recreational lease, common element for over two hundred units, and governed by a President's Council. And my Martin County Condo is part of a master association with additional sub associations.

Standard Document Pricing

I must confess. the standard document pricing is my idea only. No Florida condominium association attorney's group has adopted standard doc pricing, yet. However, the world is changing quickly. For example, SCOTUS rethinking Roe v. Wade after 58 years.

Standard documents start on the day they are adopted, respecting Florida and Federal law, but adopting stricter rules, when our federal and state elected officials have not made the changes deemed necessary to prevent another Surfside. Expunging the old rules as if they no longer existed, and archiving the old rules for historians who may want to research how we lived in the olden days.

Current pricing for updating condominium association documents seems to be around $8,000 for a plain vanilla, no frills update; more when there are unusual circumstances to navigate, perhaps around $10,000.

My proposal: discount the standard documents by 50% when the condominium association agrees to an annual update for 5% of the original cost for the next ten years, and includes a 20% discount on any and all other legal work for the condominium association.

This guarantees the condominium association attorney an ongoing relationship with the condominium association. If the relationship is good as I expect it will be, both parties will benefit. The condo board will feel comfortable consulting with the attorney when the problem seems to have a legal component. The attorney will have an opportunity to update condo docs annually, with standard updates, reflecting changes to Federal, Florida state, county and municipal statutes, as well as current thinking if the legislature is lagging behind.

Declaration of Condominium

Multi-Member Limited Liability Company

The Florida Department of State (sunbiz.org) gives guidance on the legal structure of establishing a legal structure for a condominium association. In my professional opinion, a multi-member limited liability association honors the cooperative business model advocated by Dr. Martin Luther King Jr.

Definition of Declaration of Condominium

The declaration of condominium establishes the legal structure of the association community, whose purpose is to manage common or shared property, protect owners' property values, provide services to residents, and develop a sense of community through social activities and amenities.

Condominium Professionals Collaborating

Establishing a standard declaration of condominium will mean that professionals, who are used to working independently in their own silos, will have to collaborate, cooperate and negotiate fairly with each other for the benefit of community association members.

All the community association professionals live somewhere in Florida, often in condominium associations. Or some community association professionals may live in single-family homes because they have decided that they are unwilling to give up their privacy and other things they hold dear they hold dear, like two golden retriever dogs. At any rate, condominium association professionals know the rules and have pondered the issues personally.

Taxable Status

A multi-member limited liability company is not a 501(c non-profit, which is a good thing in my professional opinion. Most revenues come from condo fees, which are non-taxable, and are used to pay annual operating expenses. The objective is to have annual operating revenues equal annual operating expenses. In reality, that seldom happens, but the profit or loss reported on a member's tax return will be minimal.

More important, *SB 4D* requires reserves to be funded by 2024, at least for buildings over three stories. For example, one Martin County Over 55 Condo has a reserve budget of $1,220,000, which must be covered by 106 residential units, or approximately $11,500 per unit.

The reserve budget is the condo savings account, which "runs with the land." Ideally it will be reported on a Title Insurance Document, with the buyer paying the seller for the amount of the condo document, as reported on an estoppel certificate when the property is sold or transferred to heirs or otherwise disposed of.

Florida Sales Tax and Use Tax

The developer should apply for a Florida sales and use tax number in the county where he/she registers the condominium documents, and transfer the Florida sales and use tax number to the condominium association on turnover.

Sales Tax

The association's accountant or its CPA firm can give guidance when sales tax should be charged. Most common instance is catering. Perhaps the women's club sells box lunches for $10.00 to raise money for the condominium community clubhouse. The $10.00 is subject to sales tax, the same as any restaurant meal.

Use Tax

Florida requires folks to report and pay use taxes on taxable items which the seller did not charge sales tax, usually because the seller is from out of state. Most condominium associations hire vendors and vendor services are almost never taxable. The vendors typically order supplies and pay the sales tax before billing the condominium association.

One word of caution - never cheat the tax man!

Articles of Incorporation

The Articles of Incorporation are prescribed by Florida Statues Chapter 605. There are only two real choices, which are allowed by Section 605.0201. Is the condominium association manager-managed or member-managed. To translate:

- Managed by a CAM Business, or a License Community Association Manager (LCAM).

OR

- Self-managed

By Laws

The very mention of bylaws in a board meeting is usually met with dread. It typically means either that a conflict has risen to the point where the bylaws must be consulted, or it means that someone is pointing out an area of noncompliance that has gone unnoticed for years. This Checklist points out the necessary elements in bylaws.

Beth Brooks, CAE, National Association of Women in Construction (NAWIC), Texas

Beth's Bylaws Checklist (Appendix A) is the clearest and most comprehensive I have seen. Still I can see some conflicts with Florida condominium law.

The development of standard condominium by-laws should be a top priority for the collaborative group of condominium professionals. Beth suggests bare bones condominium by-laws, with details kept elsewhere, perhaps the Rules and Regulations.

Rules and Regulations

Florida Condominium Association Rules & Regulations

"There are many advantages to condominium ownership in Florida. Many people enjoy the amenities, community resources, and to some extent, the rules. Anyone who has ever lived in a condominium association in Florida is well aware that the condominium association Rules and Regulations can be a serious point of contention. Rules and Regulations are necessary and without them in a condominium association, chaos would reign supreme. The last thing anyone needs, is a condominium living situation akin to Lord of the Flies.

However, there are always going to be those certain nit-picky rules that many condominium owners view as unnecessary or intrusive into their use and enjoyment of their individual condominium unit. Many residents become quite annoyed with parking rules, notice of overnight guest rules, and overly restrictive pet regulations, just to name a few. Usually such Rules and Regulations are valid and each condominium resident must adhere to them. Sometimes, on occasion Rules and Regulations may be enacted improperly."

- Ryan S. Shipp, Esquire, Law Offices of Ryan S. Shipp

Local Business Tax Receipts

Live/ Work/ Eat/ Pray/ Play

The pandemic taught us that our housing had to serve all our needs. Now that offices are opening up folks are not ready to commute five days a week to an office. Maybe a day or two a week with the option to work remotely the other days or some other schedule.

The application for a Local Business Tax Receipt (BTR) on the Martin County Tax Collector's website clearly states that a home-based business is allowed. Pre-pandemic code enforcement slapped violations on association members who conducted business from their association apartments, a scarlet letter for those folks with the audacity to disobey the rules.

The City of Stuart and the Martin County staff were so helpful in answering my questions and helping me to decipher what I needed for my myriad of small businesses. I am grateful to be in Florida and not "up north" where dodgy stuff is happening, as companies and individuals are fleeing to the sunshine.

My hope is that BIG COMPANIES will do the right thing and pay local business tax receipts for their employees who work from home. And perhaps issue short-term local business tax receipts for employees who vacation in Florida.

The extra revenue helps expand the budget for local municipalities so they can provide even better services for full-time and vacationing Floridians.

How Will Condo Reforms Work?

Prominent condo-law attorney William Sklar, of Miami-based Carlton Fields, who chaired the Florida Bar's task force, said the Legislature did not tackle a key issue -- the financial consequences of stricter inspection and reserve rules on condo owners and associations. Post-Surfside reports by the state's legal bar and other groups urged legislators to consider financial assistance for older condos with residents on fixed incomes who may find it unaffordable to build reserves or pay for extensive inspections or repairs, especially if they had waived the requirements to set aside cash.

- Andres Viglucci, Miami Herald, May 27, 2022

Overview

The legislation only applies to high rise condominiums, defined as three stories and higher. However, nervous buyers and their attorneys will be looking at any deal closely. In my professional opinion, every condominium board needs to put a plan together that can be given to buyers and realtors ASAP.

Never Waive

Remove the word WAIVE from Florida Statutes forever.

Privacy

Prospective purchasers and current condominium owners and residents should clearly understand that they give up rights to privacy when they choose to live in a condominium association. Folks that don't like the rules will be much happier in a single family home that is not part of a community association.

In a condominium like Champlain Towers South, I recommend an electronic sign-in/ sign-out at every point of entrance and egress. This would also include a gym, community pool, parking lot, golf course and any other condominium common element.

Residents must be required to check-in and check-out guests with names and ages to the condominium so that it is possible to do a head count in the event of a hurricane, a tornado or other major weather event.

Cars in the parking garage must be registered, parked in their assigned spot and electronically monitored coming and leaving the parking garage. When a car is in for repairs and the owner resident has a loaner, the loaner must be registered for the time it is there. Any changes in cars in the parking garage must be registered.

Animals that are allowed should be clearly identified in condominium Rules and Regulations as service animals, emotional support animals or just pets, by type, size, weight, etc. These animals must be registered to the owner or residents apartment. If the owner goes on vacation and another owner resident cares for the animal, this must be noticed in the security system.

The system must update immediately to the security guard's station so they may evaluate the situation in the event of an emergency situation.

There are many systems available already so it should not be hard to find one to meet the needs of every condominium association.

Federal Government - Fanny and Freddie

See the *Condominium Mortgage Industry* section

Florida Property & Casualty Insurance

See *Insurance Reform* section

Building Inspections

Qualified building inspectors, both private and municipal, are already in demand and may not be available to condominiums with smaller budgets. Condo boards need to appoint a committee to "walk the property" on a regular basis, noting any problems and reporting them to the property manager to determine how to resolve the issue[s].

Financial Accounting Records

See *Compilation, Review or Audit* section

Create New Neighborhood Condominium Associations

Smaller condominium associations are already buckling under the costs to update their documents and learn all the new rules and regulations. Some may already have a recreation lease or a master association, and sub-associations can band together to hire the professionals they need, while reducing costs.

For those small associations that seem to be without an anchor, perhaps a veterans, fraternal, religious or civic organization would consider taking several small associations under their wing, using Dr. King's cooperative business model. These community organizations generally have spaces for socializing and are vested in caring for their communities. I am guessing that members of small condominium associations may already be members of one or more of these organizations so the transition would be a natural progression.

Most of these organizations suffered income loss during the pandemic and could use income from serving as a master association for several small condominiums. This is one of the few instances where everyone wins.

Development and Construction

The Florida Legislature put new requirements on developers, which I never imagined they would so my ideas may be obsolete already. And I will include them here so you can decide.

Check out *New Norms for Florida Construction*

Working From Home

Check out *Home-based Businesses*

The Community Chest

I am pretty sure this is a new idea, but who knows. I keep seeing the crazy Monopoly Guy.

Check out *The Community Chest*

Condominium Mortgage Industry

Fannie Mae and Freddie Mac already have a questionnaire which must be completed before they will buy a mortgage in the secondary market. Board Certified Condominium and Planned Development Law attorney Lisa Anne Magill suggests having the condominium association's attorney answer the letter, highlighting the actions the specific condominium association is taking to assure building safety.

My Recommendations

Immediately call a special members meeting, properly noticed, respecting all dates and providing time for owners to speak.

The only agenda item: ask the condominium member to approve putting a lien on each owner's condominium unit based on 100% of current reserve calculation.

For example, one Martin County Over 55 Condo has a reserved budget of $1,220,000, which must be covered by 106 residential units, or approximately $11,500 per unit.

This is the condo savings account, which "runs with the land." Ideally it will be reported on a Title Insurance Document, with the buyer paying the seller for the amount of the condo document, as reported on an estoppel certificate when the property is sold or transferred to heirs or otherwise disposed of.

Condominium owners would have ten years, interest free, to pay up and remove the lien.

Or they could:

- Pay 100% cash up front

- Pay some combination of cash and lien, with the balance calculated quarterly, and adjusted to closing date, for the estoppel certificate.

In the event of a natural catastrophe—a hurricane, tornado, etc.—which may require major renovations to the condominium property, a condominium association can go to a reputable Community Association Bank and get a quick turnaround on loan for emergency repairs.

Insurance Reform

All Floridians Pay For Surfside

The $1 billion settlement for Champlain Towers South came almost entirely from insurance policies, a major reason for the increase in property and casualty rates this year. Let me be clear, I am grateful that the funds are available to provide monetary compensation for the 98 people who died in their homes, as well as the survivors who can now move on with their lives.

I am also grateful that our elected officials have taken action to stop the bleed. Our elected officials have told us that it will be 12 to 18 months before we see a leveling off of insurance premiums and then possibly some decreases if Florida is spared major weather events in the next couple of years.

My Recommendations

- Increase the deductible on your P&C Insurance. Set up a separate account and begin funding each year.

- Approve and implement a 100% reserve as described in the section on Condominium Mortgage Industry

Compilation, Review or Audit

The Financial Reporting sections of *Chapters 718 Condominiums, 719 Cooperatives, 721 Vacation and Time Share Plans and 723 Mobile Home Park Lot Tenancies, Florida Statutes* need to be updated to reflect current requirements of community association members and the insurance and mortgage industries.

I came to this conclusion after reading articles, watching videos and listening to podcasts about the Surfside Condo Tragedy. Dodgy accounting and corrupt building inspectors gave Champlain Towers South a Certificate of Occupancy in 1981 when critical components failed the building code.

Currently, cash basis statements are okay up to $150,000 in revenues, compilation $150,000 - $300,000, review $300,000 to $500,000 and audit over $500,000.

The Certified Public Accounting Profession has gotten sloppy over the years and it seems the regulators agree with me.

This from Dave Michael at the Wall Street Journal.

> "Regulators are carrying out a sweeping investigation of conflicts of interest at the nation's largest accounting firms, asking whether consulting and other non-audit services they sell undermine their ability to conduct independent reviews of public companies' financials, according to people familiar with the matter.
>
> The Securities and Exchange Commission probe highlights the agency's new focus on financial-market gatekeepers such as accountants, bankers and lawyers. These firms help companies raise capital and communicate with shareholders, but also have

duties under federal investor-protection laws. Auditors are a shareholder's first line of defense against sloppy or dodgy accounting." - Big Four Accounting Firms Come Under Regulator's Scrutiny, March 22, 2022.

Recommendations For Change

Compilations, Reviews and Audits

In the chapter on reserves, I recommend reserves at 100% of "rebuild to code reserves", which almost always is higher than replacement cost reserves. I also recommend that the reserve requirement can never be waived.

Reserves and operating budget are added together to determine if a complication, review or audit is required. This would mean that many, perhaps most, associations would be required to have an audit—increasing expenses even more when rampaging inflation is already increasing operating costs and reserves to astronomical levels.

Therefore I recommend increasing the following for associations which employ a management company (CAM Business). These levels are firm and can never be waived.

- Cash basis statements are never okay

- Compilation - up to $2 million in revenues

- Review - $2 million to $5 million in revenues

- Audit - over $5 million

All self-managed associations would be required to have an audit.

Nicole Johnson CPA, Partner, Hafer LLC, presented "What to expect during an audit," as one of the free education programs Campbell offers each month. Nicole has 18 years 'experience in HOA and condominium association management.

Campbell Property Management's services include,

> **"Annual Audit** – Campbell recommends an independent CPA firm to conduct an annual audit, review or compilation of the Association's finances."

Campbell provides most of the financial and accounting services for association clients so recommending an independent CPA could be construed as a potential conflict of interest until you factor in Campbell's strong moral compass.

Campbell Property Management is required to have an Annual Audit. The auditors will test administrative and financial systems as part of their review of internal controls. If the auditors find something that concerns them, they will discuss with Campbell's Owners and resolve their concerns before issuing their Annual Audit Report.

New Norms For Florida Construction

Vulture developers are circling, watching as municipalities start looking closely at older community association buildings, particularly those closest to the ocean.

Vulture developers buy out the community association owners at prices that seem outrageously high until the sellers look to buy into another community association in their local community. Only then do the sellers realize that they cannot afford to buy locally and much move away from their beloved community.

The residents of the newly constructed community association high rises on the beach can afford top dollar for the services they need, but the workers to provide those services have moved away, driven out by the high rents.

A vicious circle, creating chaos for working class individuals and families. How did it start?

History: Champlain Towers South

A group of Canadian businessmen came to Surfside in the 1970s with a vision of bringing luxury high-rise developments to the sleepy oceanfront town on the northern border of Miami Beach. Their first project, Champlain South, was plagued by problems, starting with a building moratorium that was lifted only when developers pledged $200,000 to update the town's aging sewer system.

The first general contractor on the project resigned. A second also had to be replaced. And construction was temporarily halted mid-project by a cease-and-desist order, issued as the town debated the last-minute addition of a 13th-story penthouse on one side of the tower. The condo was designed by architect William M. Friedman and structural engineer Sergio Breiterman — a duo with histories of cutting corners.

A few years earlier, Breiterman oversaw the design and construction of a parking garage, built with inadequate rebar, that began failing nearly the same day it was completed. Friedman's license had once been suspended for "gross incompetence" after he designed two billboards that blew over in a hurricane.

— Monica Richardson, Executive Editor of the Miami Herald

Future Change: Radical Surgery

Now is the perfect time to create change by performing radical surgery. Great jobs with great benefits are going unfilled because there are not enough skilled workers that want the available jobs.

Our education system produced too many liberal arts PhDs and not enough engineers and professional tradespeople, the folks who make our world work. That is changing as high schoolers begin to realize that the education colleges and universities are offering is not worth the cost of student debt. Students today want to graduate with ZERO debt. Florida colleges and universities need to make that possible.

Florida colleges and universities, among the best in the United States, are realizing that they must train students for jobs which will pay middle class wages on graduation, enough for a graduate to save for a home, get married and start a family or pursue some other equally worthy goal. And, of course, no student debt.

The construction industry is a great place to start. Vanish the vulture developers, back to Canada or Silicon Valley or whatever. Florida needs developers, general contractors, construction lenders, etc. who grew up in Florida, know the landscape and Florida law, and are passionate about building the best live/ work/ eat/ play/ pray homes for fellow Floridians.

Basic Requirements for Executive Positions on Florida Community Association Development Teams

- Five years Florida residency of six months and one day

- Florida driver's license

- Personal vehicle registered in Florida

- Registered to vote in the State of Florida

- Personal residence in membership association in the Florida

- No professional license suspensions, in Florida or elsewhere

- Five years 'experience working as a tradesperson on a Florida community association development team

Developer's Responsibilities From First Sale to Turnover

Build the best building(s) possible, following the Florida Building Code which is among the best in the country, sourcing materials locally whenever possible and never cutting corners.

Never waive anything, even when allowed by Florida statutes.

Home Based Businesses

My Home-based Businesses

COVID 19 did one good thing. It made Live/ Work/ Eat/ Play/ Pray legal. I am so happy about that, but some folks may not be, particularly if they have a large family and were forced to coexist in one space for almost two years.

I moved to Stuart on May 8, 2020, because the City of Lake Worth Beach branded me as a scarlet woman for running a home-based business out of my condo apartment. I assimilated slowly into my condominium community in Stuart, determined to not repeat the disaster in Lake Worth Beach.

Unfortunately, my expertise was recognized by the board member who was assigned to interview me in order to be accepted into the community by signing the estoppel certificate. I was asked to serve on the board and, like an idiot, I accepted. I didn't last long and I noticed the woman who replaced me as secretary is no longer secretary.

Soon after I became an LCAM and registered Freancy & Company LLC as an CAM business, I marched myself down to Stuart City Hall to inquire about home-based businesses. The folks in the Local Business Tax Office helped me fill out the forms and in no time I was legally in business in Stuart and Martin County. And since I am well over sixty-five years old, all fees were waived.

I also registered my publishing business, Emerson House Press, and my virtual art gallery, Emerson House Art Gallery, with all fees waived.

The next step for Stuart and Martin County is to get companies with employees who work from home to pay local business taxes for each and every employee that works even one day a week from home.

The Community Chest

Now that I can legally do business in my condo, I want to show my appreciation to my fellow condominium members, some who are still reeling from increases in condo fees as we are experiencing the worst inflation in over 40 years.

I propose paying 1% of all my business revenues into a fund called the Martin County Over 55 Condo Community Chest. You may have heard of 1% for the Planet®. This is similar but much closer to home.

The funds would be available to Martin County Over 55 condominium owners who are experiencing temporary or permanent financial distress.

A committee of the Martin County Over 55 Women's Club would be ideal. The Committee members would have to be permanent residents since they would be required to meet in person with individuals in distress, and hurricane season (June 1 to November 30) is generally the most stressful time of the year.

To honor Dr. King's cooperative business model, community chest loans would need to be repaid whenever possible. Permanent community chest loans would operate like a reserve mortgage; temporary loan to be repaid in one year.

I imagine the Community Chest fund would grow very quickly as more condo members register their home based businesses and begin contributing to the fund.

Appendices

Appendix A: Beth's Bylaws Checklist

The very mention of bylaws in a board meeting is usually met with dread. It typically means either that a conflict has risen to the point where the bylaws must be consulted, or it means that someone is pointing out an area of noncompliance that has gone unnoticed for years. This Checklist points out the necessary elements in bylaws.

Because regulations about nonprofit bylaws are done individually by state (rather than the federal government) there is quite a bit of variation. For example, some states regulate the number of board members. It's important to obtain the applicable state laws and make sure that the bylaws are in compliance.

Three overall guiding principles for nonprofit bylaws:

Don't put too much in the bylaws. If you specify a board committee in the bylaws, for instance, and there hasn't been such a committee in a few years, someone could claim that you are in violation of your own bylaws. Or, along the same lines, if the bylaws state that meetings will be held on the third Wednesday of each month, you can't change to Thursdays without a change in the bylaws.

Remember that if trouble erupts -- such as internal conflict or attacks from others -- the bylaws will become very important. So make sure they are reviewed approximately every three years. Because board officer terms make it hard for the board to keep track of bylaw revisions, make sure that all Board members receive Board orientation and that the bylaws are not only discussed, but reviewed .

Immediately note any changes made to the bylaws. Too often everyone forgets about changes to the bylaws. Placing an amended date along with the changes keeps everyone up to date. Appropriate changes to the bylaws should be recorded in the board minutes, and reviewed by an attorney experienced in nonprofit law.

Here is a checklist to ensure the most important provisions are included in your bylaws.

Indemnification. A statement that limits the personal liability of board members.

Membership guidelines: Whether the organization has individual members (such as professional association) or organizational membership or hybrid, state the qualifications for membership what their rights are. For example, in a true membership organization, members have the right to elect officers. Even if you don't have members with legally enforceable membership rights such as voting rights, you can still have people called "members," but the distinction should be clarified in the bylaws.

Number of board members. Example: a set number of board members, or minimum of five and a maximum of fifteen board members. Some states specify a minimum, and some specify a formula for a minimum and maximum, so check your state's law.

Quorum: A quorum is the minimum number of board members who must be present for official decisions to be made. For example, if an organization currently has fifteen members, and the bylaws state that one-third of the members constitutes a quorum, then official decisions can only be made at board meetings where five or more members are present.

Terms and term limits. Example: two years, with term limits of three consecutive terms (making a total of six years). Note any restrictions once they have served on the board. For example, after a year off, a board member may be permitted to return. Similarly, terms can be staggered so that, for instance, one-third of the board is up for reelection each year.

Define Officers: Spell out the titles of officers, how the officers are appointed or elected, their terms and what they do. Example: appointed by majority vote at a regular meeting of the board; an officer term is for one year. There should also be job descriptions of the officers.

Procedure for **removing a board member** or officer. Example: by majority vote at a regularly scheduled meeting where the item was placed on the written agenda distributed at least two weeks ahead.

Conflict of interest policy. Some bylaws simply state that there will be a conflict of interest policy but keep its exact wording out of the bylaws.

Minimum number of board meetings per year. Example: four, with one in each quarter.

How a special or **emergency board meeting** may be called.

How a committee may be created or dissolved.

What committees exist, how members are appointed, and responsibilties, if any

Conference calls and electronic meetings. Example: votes by e-mail or online are allowed. Meetings may be held by conference call. Many boards are adding sections to the bylaws that allow holding a board meeting via Skype or other meeting platforms.

Each board member should be given a copy of the articles of incorporation, the IRS and state determination letters, and the bylaws. Some organizations also post their bylaws on a password-protected section of their website.

Beth Brooks, CAE
Executive Vice President NAWIC
Beth@texas.net
512 633 9943

INSPIRATIONS FOR COMMUNITY ACTION

Diane Freaney
Rooted Investing, LLC
Portland, Oregon USA

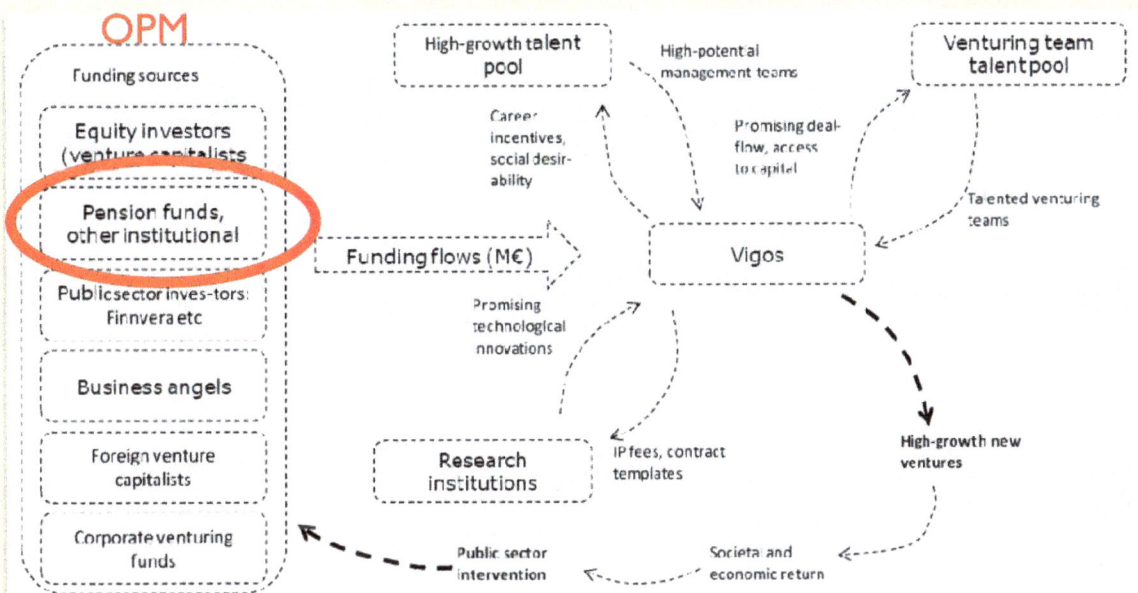

OPM

Funding sources

Equity investors (venture capitalists

Pension funds, other institutional

Public sector inves-tors: Finnvera etc

Business angels

Foreign venture capitalists

Corporate venturing funds

High-growth talent pool

High-potential management teams

Venturing team talent pool

Career incentives, social desir-ability

Promising deal-flow, access to capital

Funding flows (M€)

Vigos

Talented venturing teams

Promising technological innovations

IP fees, contract templates

High-growth new ventures

Research institutions

Public sector intervention

Societal and economic return

Figure 4 Anticipated Dynamic of the New Venture Accelerator Field

67

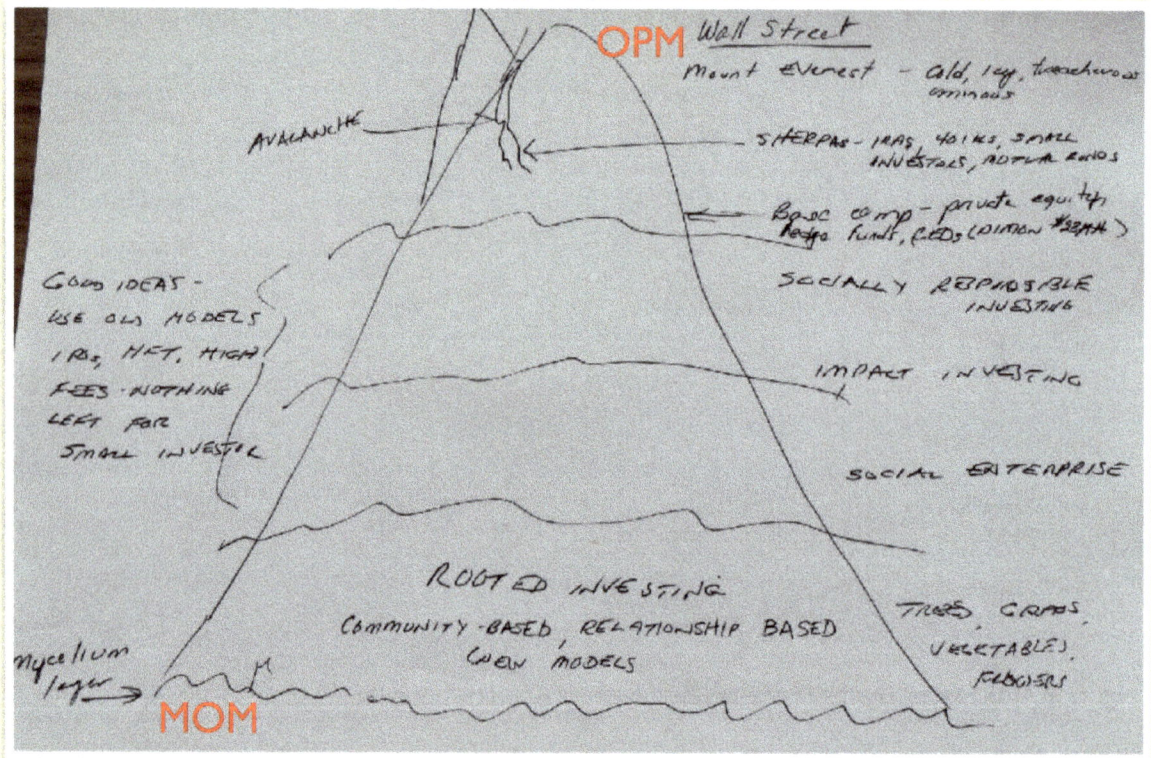

OPM
OTHER PEOPLES MONEY

MOM
MY OWN MONEY

OPM	MOM
COMPLEX	SIMPLE
EXPERT	DIY
NUMBERS	PEOPLE
GLOBAL	LOCAL

BEST RETIREMENT
INVESTMENT
IS
YOUR HOME,
YOUR COMMUNITY.

COMMUNITY AS HOME

more than a house…

Robin Corbo, muralist

storytime by
Nikki Brown Clown

Handmade Dolls by Nikki

Artist-In-Residence Wynde Dyer, Tarp Quilt Artist

Resources

Introduction to Resources

The resources I read/ watched/ listened to became very clear in the months after the Surfside Condo Tragedy on June 24, 2021.

The Miami Herald has stayed focused on the local community and produced some amazing journalism. A 12-part investigative journalism podcast coproduced with Treefort Media, Collapse: Disaster in Surfside, and an interactive reconstruction of the collapse, House of Cards: How Decades of Problems Converged The Night Champlain Towers Fell.

If you live in a Florida community association now, or are considering moving to one in the future, I encouraged you to devour everything from the *Miami Herald*. The Florida legislature may be willing to "kick the can down the road," but the insurance and mortgage industries, the attorneys, accountants and property managers and other professionals community association owners and residents depend on are already crafting their own rules.

In my opinion, the Surfside Condo Tragedy would not have been possible if current state and local rules and regulations were in place in 1981.

Miami Herald

These are the stories the Pulitzer Prize committee considered before awarding the *Miami Herald* its 23rd Pulitzer Prize, this one in Breaking News:

Blaskey, Sarah and Albright, Aaron. Two days before condo collapse, a pool contractor photographed this damage in garage. January 25, 2022. (Originally published June 28, 2021)

Blaskey, Sarah and Albright, Aaron. After the collapse of Surfside's Champlain tower: a day of dread, helplessness, heroism. January 25, 2022. (Originally published June 24, 2021)

Blaskey, Sarah and Al-Jamea, Sohail. See where experts identified an 'initiation point' of the condo collapse -- in the garage. January 25, 2022. (Original published July 2, 2021)

Dolven, Taylor and Ogle, Connie. Here are the names and stories of the missing and dead in Surfside condo collapse. July 2, 2021. (Originally published June 25, 2021)

Pitchon, Allie, Wile, Rob, Gross, Samantha J., Flechas, Joey. 'The apartments were gone.' Survivors recount harrowing escape from collapsed condo. November 4, 2021. (Originally published June 24, 2021)

Sheinerman, Marie-Rose, Gross, Samantha J., Padro, Ocasio, Bianca, Hanks, Douglas, Chang, Daniel. 99 feared missing in rubble of collapsed condo in Surfside as search, vigil continue. November 4, 2021. (Originally published June 24, 2021)

Other Miami Herald Stories

Blakey, Sarah and Conarck, Ben. Surfside condo was 'screaming' as an alarming crack formed just weeks before the collapse. May 14, 2022.

Blaskey, Sarah, Nehamas, Nicholas, Conarck, Ben and Leibowitz, Aaron. '[Bleep] that wall,' contractor said when vibrations near Surfside condo got 'too high'. April 18, 2022.

Ceballos, Ana. Five things to know about the Florida Legislature's proposed condominium reforms. Miami Herald. May 25, 2022.

Cutout, Devoun and Wile, Rob. North Miami Beach orders 10-story condo evacuated after report declares it unsafe. July 7, 2021.

Florida's shameful lack of condo-safety laws on the brink of change after Surfside. Miami Herald Editorial Board. March 1, 2022.

Hanks, Douglas. A mystery no more? Condominium financial reports are close to becoming public in Miami-Dade. March 1, 2022.

Klas, Mary Ellen. Many condo owners can't agree on funding reserves for repairs. Legislature can't, either. March 11, 2022.

Kurtz, Nicole R. Federal and state reforms necessary to address Florida's residential insurance woes. Miami Herald. May 20, 2022.

Robertson, Linda. $83 million Surfside settlement endorsed by judge but some victims plan to object. March 11, 2022.

Vassalo, Martin and Leibowitz, Aaron. 60-unit building in North Miami Beach ordered evacuated, 'structurally unsound'. April 4, 2022.

Vassalo, Martin and Weaver, Jay. 'My mom is priceless.' What relatives of Surfside collapse victims said after settlement. May 12, 2022.

Vassalo, Martin. 'Do not forget.' Surfside hangs banners along collapse site honoring 98 victims. May 14, 2022.

Vassalo, Martin. Surfside condo collapse site to be sold for $120 million to Dubai developer, no other bids. May 20, 2022.

Vassolo, Martin, Weaver, Jay and Robertson, Linda. Judge in Surfside collapse lawsuit agrees to pay condo owners more for property loss. May 25, 2022.

Viglucci, Andres and Klas, Mary Ellen. Florida legislators won't require condo inspections. Here are the consequences. March 18, 2022.

Viglucci, Andres. After Surfside tragedy, 'a major move forward in safety.' How will condo reforms work? May 27, 2022.

Weaver, Jay and Robertson, Linda. Defendants' payments detailed as lawyers submit $1B Surfside settlement to judge. May 27,2022,

Weaver, Jay. For families, dividing $1 billion Surfside condo settlement looms as 'extremely painful'. May 15, 2022.

Wall Street Journal

Eisen, Ben and Friedman, Nicole. Surfside Tower Collapse Makes Buying Condos More Complicated. February 20, 2022.

Michaels, Dave. Big Four Accounting Firms Come Under Regulator's Scrutiny. March 15, 2022.

Wall Street Journal Staff. What We Know About the Building Collapse in
 Surfside, Fla. July 6, 2021.

Florida Association News

"Post Surfside Update and FL Bar Recommendations." Education Webinar.
 Evan Bradley, CFO Campbell Property Management, Lisa Magill, Esq. Kaye
 Bender Rembaum, and Evan Swaysland, Swaysland Professional
 Engineering Consultants. January 19, 2022.

Wikipedia

History of the legal profession,
 https://en.wikipedia.org/wiki/History_of_the_legal_profession

Structural engineering,
 https://en.wikipedia.org/wiki/Structural_engineering

Sunset Park, Brooklyn,
 https://en.wikipedia.org/wiki/Sunset_Park,_Brooklyn#Ethnic_groups

Other Resources

Blanch, Roberto C. The Path Forward for Florida Condo-Safety Reforms.
 Florida HOA Lawyer Blog. April 22, 2022.

Hurttibise, Ron. Fears mount that many insurers might not be financially
 prepared for hurricane season, despite reforms. South Florida Sun-
 Sentinel. May 28, 2022.

Jacobs, Jane. The Death and Life of Great American Cities. New York:
 Random House, 1961.

National and State Statistical Review for 2017: Community Association. Data. Community Association Institute.

O'Brien, Doug. On Martin Luther King, Jr. Day, lifting up co-ops as a strategy for greater equity in our economy and society. NCBA CLUSA Magazine. January 20, 2020.

Poliakoff, Gary A. The Florida Condominium Act. Move Law Review. Volume 16, Issue 1, 1991, Article 15.

Sullivan, Sean. What is a 501(c)(4), anyway? Washington Post. May 13, 2013.

Wallman, Brittany et al. <u>Becker & Poliakoff law firm the 'nemesis' of condo safety reformers</u>. South Florida Sun-Sentinel. Sep 28, 2021.

Websites

Alberta Coop, https://alberta.coop/

Bal Harbour Shops: https://www.balharbourshops.com/https://youtu.be/_P6fECsSX8M

Campbell Property Management: (About) https://www.campbellpropertymanagement.com/about-us/company-history/, (Painting Projects Planning Process CEU Webinar) https://youtu.be/_P6fECsSX8M, (Request for Proposal) https://www.campbellpropertymanagement.com/request-a-proposal/

Carmela's Brick Oven Pizza and Wine Bar: https://carmelaspizza.com/

Community Association Institute: https://foundation.caionline.org/wp-content/uploads/2018/06/2017StatsReview.pdf

Connect Credit Union, https://www.connectcu.org/index.php/your-credit-union/hours-locations/martin-county-stuart

Florida Department of State, https://www.sunbiz.org

Fred Gray Systems, Inc.: https://www.graysystems.com/

Lake Harbour Towers at 801 Lake Shore Drive (Lake Park, FL): https://www.redfin.com/FL/Lake-Park/801-Lake-Shore-Dr-33403/unit-118/home/42417498

Miami Herald Surfside Investigation: https://www.miamiherald.com/news/special-reports/surfside-investigation/article256633336.html

Sea View Hotel: https://seaview-hotel.com/

Vinoy Park Hotel: https://www.marriott.com/en-us/hotels/tpasr-the-vinoy-renaissance-st-petersburg-resort-and-golf-club/overview/history-of-the-vinoy/

Addendum

Community Association Banking

I was pleasantly surprised to learn that community associations have their own relationship banking system, actually departments in large national banks. I met four relationship managers at in-person events recently. They all knew each other and encouraged me to stop by and speak with the other bankers.

All offer free lockbox, remote deposit services and interface with community association accounting systems, plus investment options for funds over the $250,000 FDIC limit and loans for construction projects. If Chaplain Towers South had access to a construction loan in 2018, tragedy may have been averted.

Popular Association Banking's website has fill-in forms making it easy to collect required information before meeting with a relationship officer. Zoom meetings are acceptable today, saving gas and travel time.

Community Association Data Sheet can be found here:
   https://documents.popular.com/pdfs/PAB/pab_datasheet.pdf

Community Association Premium Finance Program - Loan Form:
   https://documents.popular.com/pdfs/PAB/pab_finance_program.pdf

Alliance Association Bank

Lisa Elkan, EBP, VP Association Banking

Cell: 561-212-2091

21346 St. Andrews Blvd #171, Boca Raton, FL 33433

lelkan@allianceassociationbank.com

Centennial Bank

Jennifer Olson, LCAM, VP, Association Banking Relationship Manager

Tel: 561-209-7166 Cell: 561-236-3378

500 S Australian Avenue Set #100, West Palm Beach, FL 33401

jolson@my100bank.com

Popular Association Banking

Jane E. Bracken, PCAM

Tel: 954-907-1010 Fax: 305-821-7284

Deerfield Beach, FL 33442

JBracken@popular.com

TRUIST

Jayme Gelfand, SVP, Relationship Marketing Manager

Truist Association Services

9885 Glades Road, Boca Raton, FL 33434

Office: 561-251-1980 Client Care: 888-722-6669

jayme.gelfand@truist.com

Acknowledgements

In Gratitude

To Retha Mae Lowe, resident of the City of Lake Worth Beach, former commissioner for over 38 years and founder of the Jazzy Seniors. Retha Mae's husband Grady, may he rest is peace, brought his new wife a home in an area once designated as the Osborne Colored Addition (adjacent but separate from the Whites-Only area) of Lake Worth in 1976.

To Kali Amanda Browne for teaching me the art and science of self-publishing books and improving the quality of my writing dramatically.

To Nicholas Papaefthimiou, AIA, Masters Architecture and Structural Engineering, UC, Berkeley and BS Architecture and Urban Planning, MIT, principal InfillPDX and Small Homes Northwest (https://www.sightline.org/2019/12/13/a-portland-adu-program-pairs-lower-wealth-homeowners-and-low-income-tenants), for teaching me about the built environment, for his expertise and support in sorting out construction design flaws at the Emerson Street House and for inspiring me to write the book series Politics of Place.

To Mia Sheperd, former Project Manager for the Emerson Street House and general contractor Block Design Build LLC (https://blockdesignbuildllc.com), for teaching me about architecture, engineering and the built environment, and inspiring me to write the book series What Is This Place?

Author's Bio

I have been seated at the table – rather, more accurately, been seated behind the white men seated at the table and told to hold my tongue – at the launch of some of the most radical new business models of the last century.

I have had a front row seat for every new finance and/or economic theory that came down the pike.

This is a dubious honor. I have watched these same new business models crash and burn, take jobs, destroy families, make ghost towns of cities, compromise our health and well-being, and rob us of our happiness. With the economic meltdown of 2008, I watched as my retirement fund plummeted 42% percent from the top of the market in 2007 to the bottom in 2009.

My life has been magical. I have over 70 years life/work experience and an excellent educational background.

Syracuse University (1965) – In my Accounting courses, I learned to fill in forms and play games with numbers. In Anthropology and Public Speaking, I learned storytelling and gained an appreciation of other cultures.

Harvard Business School – Corporate Finance Executive Education (1982) – I learned about OPM (Other People's Money), the strategy that brought the Global Financial Markets to their knees in 2008.

University of Pennsylvania – Organizational Dynamics (1999) – I learned that student's work is only valued when it follows a structured academic path. My Master's thesis – <u>A New Model for the Creative Use of College Endowments to Reduce College Tuition</u> would have prevented today's student loan crisis. Penn had no mechanism for "the administrators" to listen to students.

Bainbridge Graduate Institute (BGI) (2013) – I learned the importance of social media to listening deeply and delivering my message.

At an early age, I learned to communicate by listening. At my current age, I feel driven to share the knowledge and understanding amassed during my lifetime. Now I am speaking out.

—Diane Freaney, CPA, LCAM 57368

Freaney & Company, LLC, CAM Business 5980

Epilogue

The story of the Collapse of Champlain Towers South is the never ending story. I have committed to releasing the e-book version of *Politics of Place: Surfside Condo Tragedy* on June 24, 2022, the first anniversary of the collapse.

And every day there is more news in the *Miami Herald*.

The most recent article in the Miami Herald, Meet the lawyer at the center of the Surfside condo case. He's patient, empathetic and exhausted, highlights the work of Michael Goldberg, the receiver handpicked by Miami-Dade Judge Michale Hanzman.

A Federal investigation by the National Institute of Standards and Technology (NIST) which is scheduled to conclude by September 30, 2024 just issued a six month update, "We have ruled nothing out: In Surfside condo collapse, findings still far away."

With so many balls in the air, it is impossible to imagine how the trajectory that the collapse has put us on will end.

I expect to be issuing regular updates for at least the next year and possibly until the NIST has completed its investigation.

Peace!

Coming Soon! Four Book Series!

What is This Place?

The **What is This Place?** book series includes the final documentation of the Living Building Challenge and the Living Community Challenge of the International Living Future Institute.

Higher Education

The **Higher Education** book series features the final projects for my graduate degree programs. I have been studying the business of higher education for over sixty years, since I was a teenager researching colleges and universities to decide where I wanted to attend. As you may be able to guess, I have strong opinions on how to bring higher education into this century.

Sally Sleuth will join the team to ferret out political lies and corruption in the higher education systems, focusing on USC, the Ivy League Colleges and Universities, and the State of Florida College and University system. Stay tuned as we dig deep on one of the biggest scandals of our time.

Complexity = Corruption

The **Complexity = Corruption** series was inspired by an *Time Magazine* article (Complexity Equals Corruption, Fareed Zakaria, published Oct. 31, 2011). The article is about the Complexity of the US Tax Code, of which Zakaria says, "The U.S. tax system is not simply corrupt; it is corrupt in a deceptive manner that has degraded the entire system of American government."

In this series we will explore corruption in Big Tech, Big Pharma, Big everything and anything. The solution is always SIMPLE. I promise a wild ride.

Politics of Place

The **Politics of Place** series started with places I have lived since I was a baby. I have delved into old family photos, photos on the Internet, and stories in my head to fill in the blanks.

Sally Sleuth will be an active partner in this series, since it is peppered with political lies and vested interests. I will leave it to Sally to work on these issues.

We Want to Hear From You

Let us know your thoughts.

Email at thecatlady@dianefreaney.com

Or Snail Mail

Diane Freaney

Emerson House Press

2336 SE Ocean Blvd #230

Stuart, FL 34996-3310